Cover photo courtesy of Photofest

ISBN-13: 978-1-4234-5183-9
ISBN-10: 1-4234-5183-X

7777 W. BLUEMOUND RD. P.O. BOX 13819 MILWAUKEE, WI 53213

Visit Hal Leonard Online at
www.halleonard.com

CONTENTS

Back in Baby's Arms

Words and Music by Bob Montgomery

Intro
Happily, with a bounce (in 2)

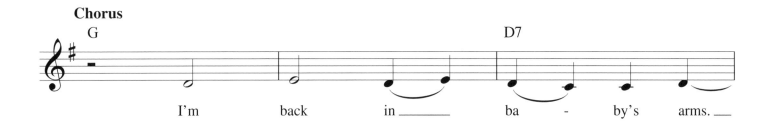

Chorus

I'm back in _____ ba - by's arms. _____

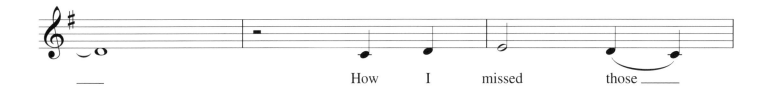

_____ How I missed those _____

lov - in' arms. I'm back where

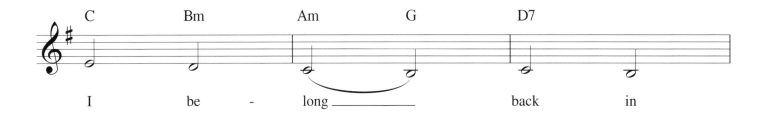

I be - long _____ back in

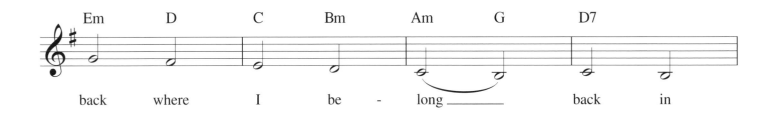

back where I be - long _____ back in

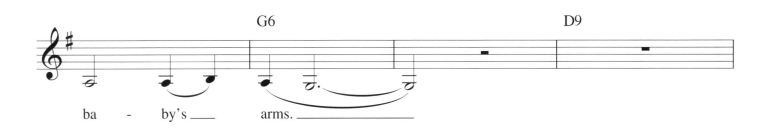

ba - by's _____ arms. _____

Verse

Thought I did - n't need _ his love _

_____ 'til he took _____ it a -

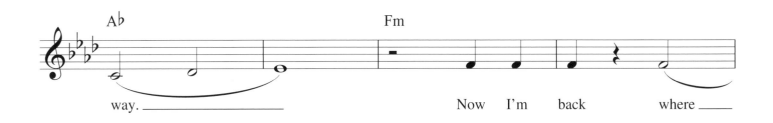

way. _____ Now I'm back where _____

_ I be - long _____ and in my ba - by's

6

Chorus

arms   I'm   gon - na   stay.   I'm

back   in _____ ba - by's   arms. _____

How   I   missed   those ____   lov - in'

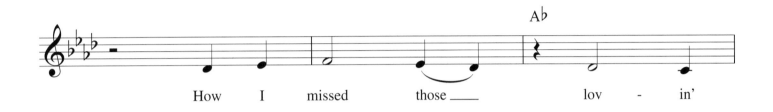

arms.   I'm   back   where

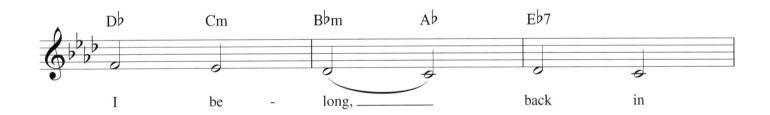

I   be - long, _____   back   in

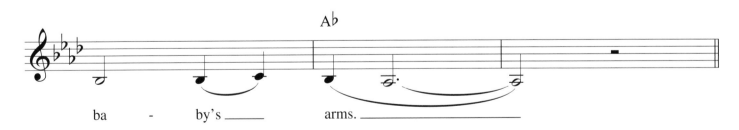

ba - by's ____   arms. _____

Outro

Fade out

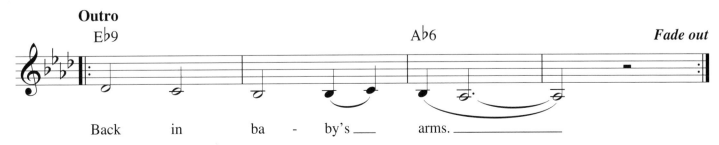

Back   in   ba - by's ____   arms. _____

Foolin' 'Round

Words and Music by Harlan Howard and Buck Owens

Intro
Brightly

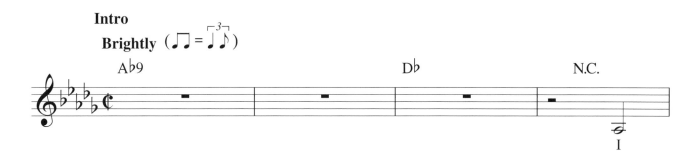

Chorus

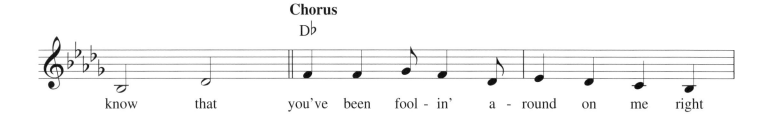

know that you've been fool-in' a-round on me right

from the start. _ So I'll give back your

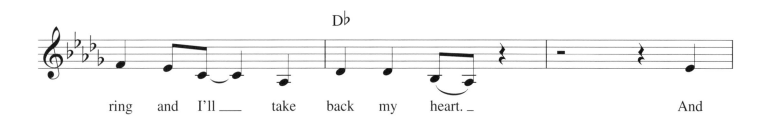

ring and I'll _ take back my heart. _ And

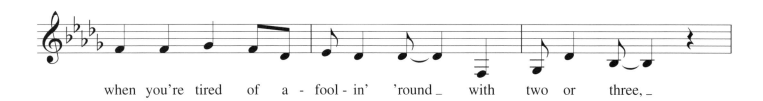

when you're tired of a-fool-in' 'round _ with two or three, _

then come on home _ and fool a-round _ with me.

Verse

Well, I was-n't fool-in' a-round the day __ I

Ab9

said "I do." __ But man-y a night __ I

Db

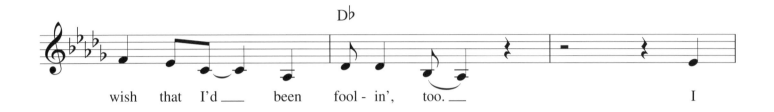

wish that I'd __ been fool-in', too. __ I

Gb

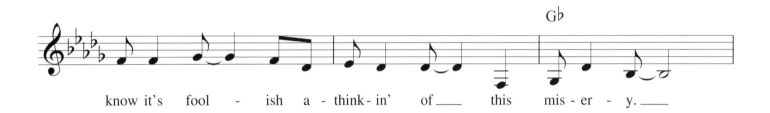

know it's fool - ish a - think-in' of __ this mis-er - y. __

Ab

But when it's you, __ a fool I'll al - ways

Db   N.C.

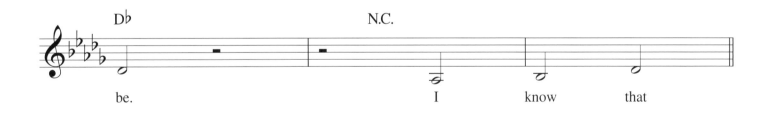

be.   I know that

Chorus

Db   Ab9

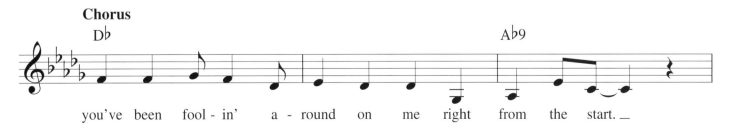

you've been fool-in' a - round on me right from the start. __

9

So I'll give back your ring and I'll ___ take

back my heart. ___ And when you're tired ___ of a -

fool - in' 'round ___ with two or three, ___ then

come on home ___ and fool a - round ___ with me.

Verse

So ___ hon - ey, fool ___ a - round you know ___ right

where I'm at. ___ And don't ___ wor - ry if I'm

lone - some 'cause ___ I'm used to that. ___ And when you're tired ___ of a -

fool - in' 'round ___ with two or three, ___ then

come on home __ and fool a - round __ with me.

Chorus

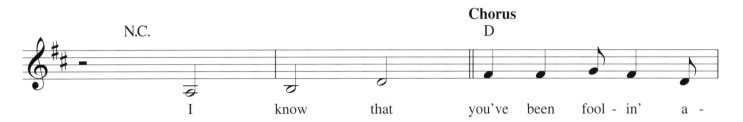

I know that you've been fool - in' a -

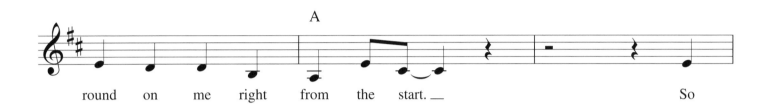

round on me right from the start. __ So

I'll give back your ring and I'll __ take back my heart. __

And when you're tired __ of a - fool - in' 'round __ with

two or three, __ then come on home __ and

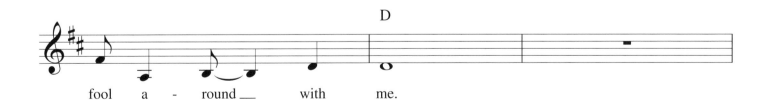

fool a - round __ with me.

Crazy

Words and Music by Willie Nelson

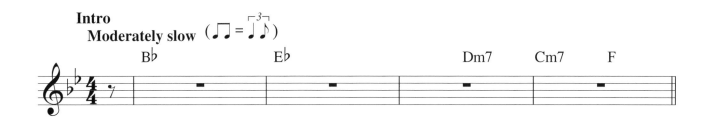

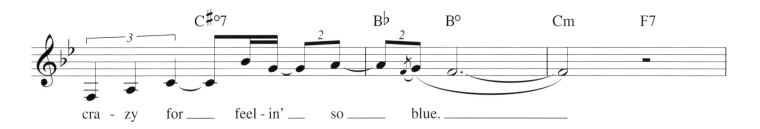

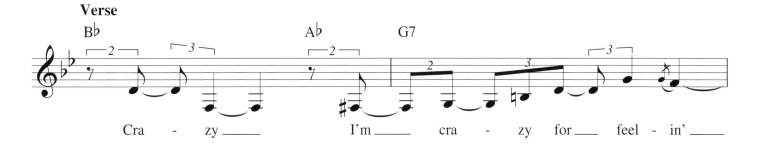

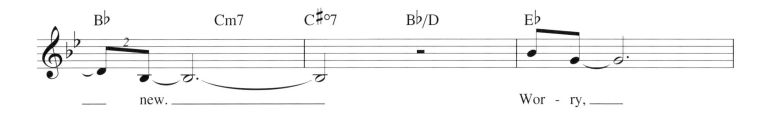

new. _____ Wor - ry, ____

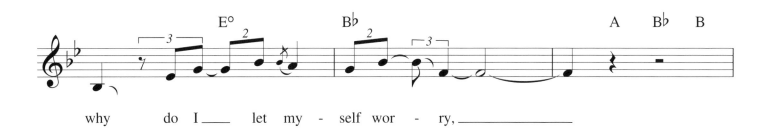

why do I ____ let my - self wor - ry, _____

won - d'rin' _ what in the world ____ did I do? _____

_____ Oh ____ cra - zy for think - in' ____ that my love ____

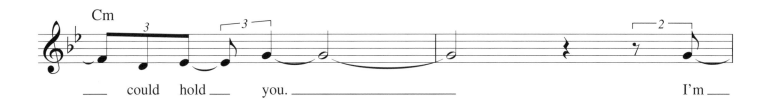

____ could hold ____ you. _____ I'm ____

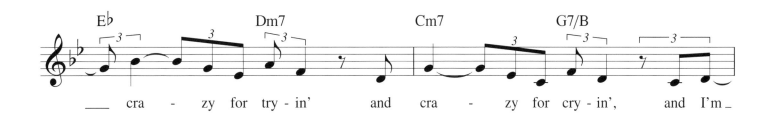

____ cra - zy for try - in' and cra - zy for cry - in', and I'm_

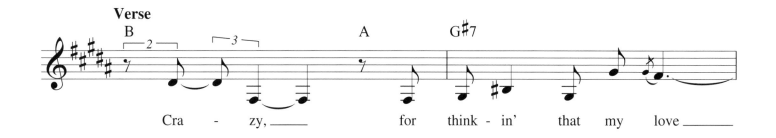

___ cra - zy for ___ lov - in' you._

Verse

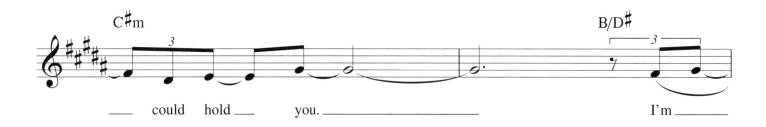

_Cra - zy, ___ for think - in' that my love _____

___ could hold ___ you. _____ I'm _____

___ cra - zy for try - in' ___ and I'm ___ cra - zy for cry - in', and I'm_

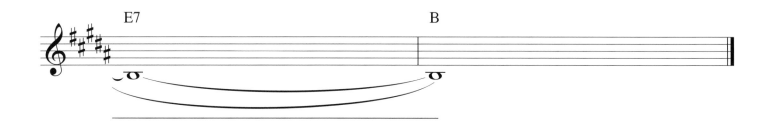

_cra - zy ___ for lov - in' you. _____

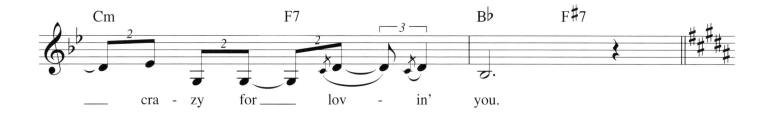

Half As Much

Words and Music by Curley Williams

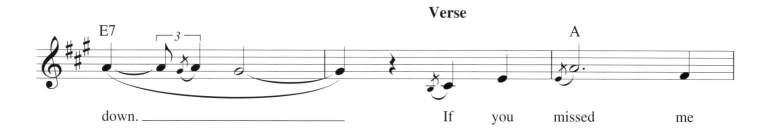

Verse

down. _____ If you missed me

half as much as I ___ miss you, ___ you would - n't

stay a - way ___ half as much as you do. _____

___ I know that ___ I ___ would nev - er be this

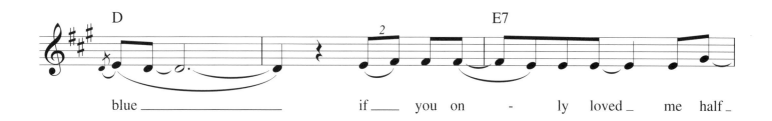

blue _____ if ___ you on - ly loved _ me half _

___ as much as I _____ loved ___ you. ___ If you

loved me half as much as I ____ love you, ____

you would-n't wor - ry me ____ half as much as you do. ____

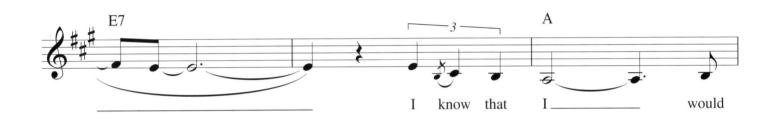

I know that I _____ would

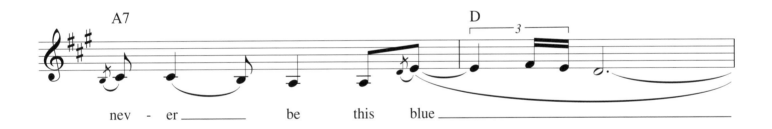

nev - er _____ be this blue _____

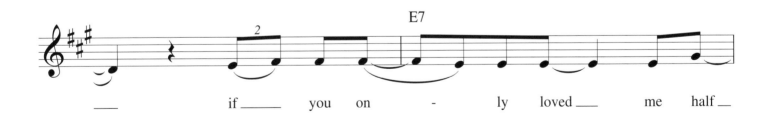

____ if ____ you on - ly loved ____ me half ____

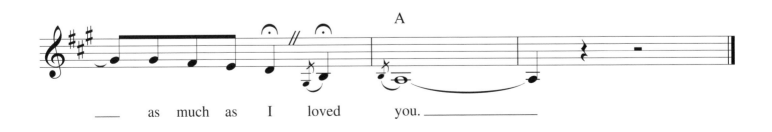

____ as much as I loved you. _____

I Fall to Pieces

Words and Music by Hank Cochran and Harlan Howard

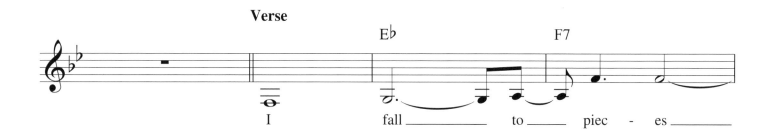

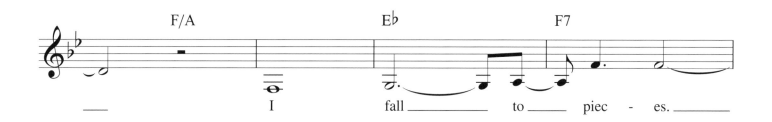

nev - er kissed. You want me to for - get, pre-tend we've

nev - er met, _____ and I've tried and I've

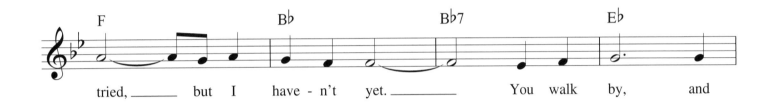

tried, _____ but I have - n't yet. _____ You walk by, and

I fall to _____ piec - es. _____

Bridge

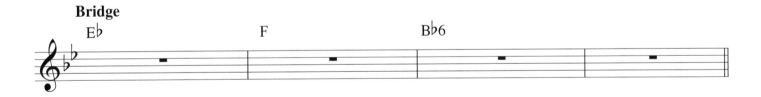

Verse

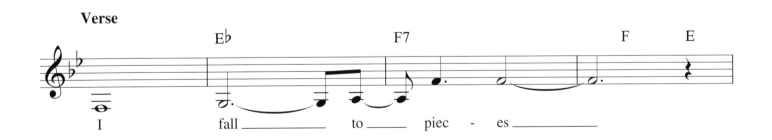

I fall _____ to _____ piec - es _____

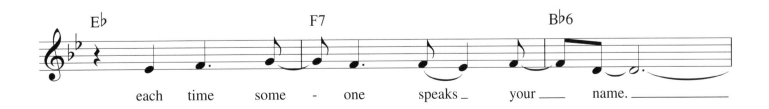

each time some - one speaks _ your ____ name. _____

She's Got You

Words and Music by Hank Cochran

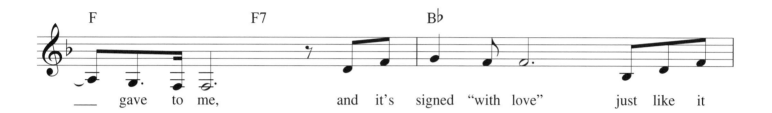

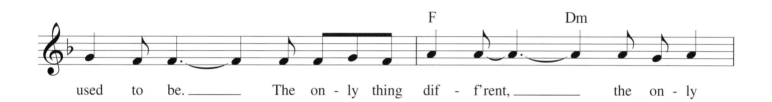

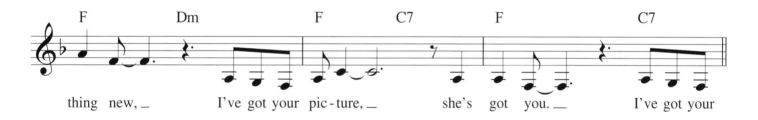

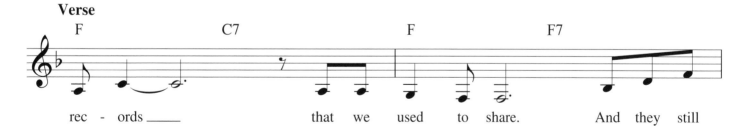

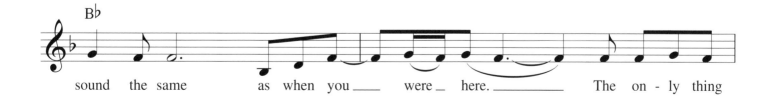

Bridge

Verse

Bridge

got you. ___ I've got your mem - o - ry, _____ or has it

got me? ___ I real - ly don't know, ___ but I know ___ it

won't let ___ me be. _____ I've got your

Verse

class ring ___ that proved you care. ___ And it still

looks the same _____ as ___ when you gave it, dear. ___ The on - ly thing

dif - f'rent, ___ the on - ly thing new, ___ I've got these

lit tle things, ___ she's ___ got ___ you.

Sweet Dreams

Words and Music by Don Gibson

Intro
Moderately

Verse

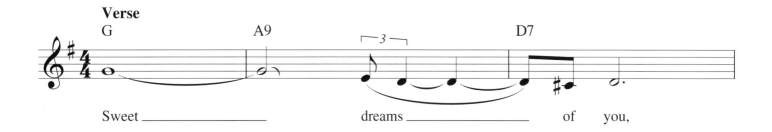

Sweet dreams of you,

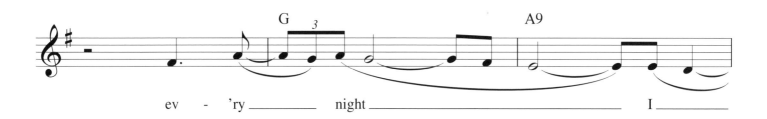

ev - 'ry night I

go through. Why can't I

for - get you and start my life a - new. In -

- stead of hav - ing sweet dreams a - bout you.

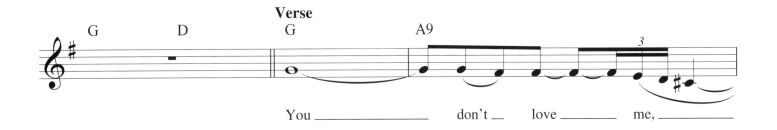

Verse

You _____ don't __ love _____ me, _____

____ it's plain. _____ I _____ should _____ know __

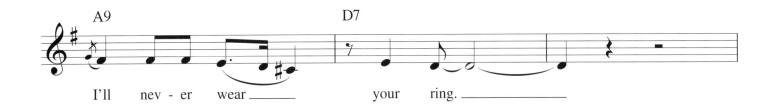

I'll nev - er wear _____ your ring. _____

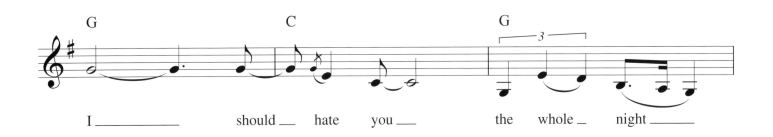

I _____ should __ hate you __ the whole __ night _____

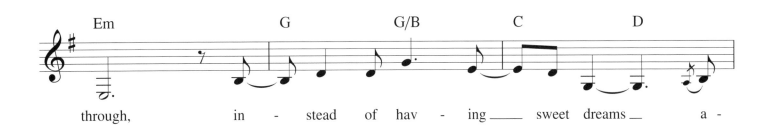

through, in - stead of hav - ing _____ sweet dreams __ a -

Verse

bout you. _____ Sweet _____

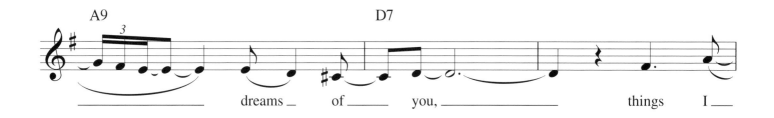

dreams _____ of _____ you, _____ things I _____

_____ know _____ can't _____ come true. ___

Why ___ can't _____ I for - get the past, start _

___ lov - ing _____ some - one new? In -

Freely

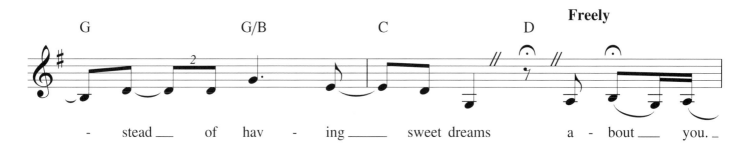

- stead ___ of hav - ing _____ sweet dreams a - bout ___ you. _

Walkin' After Midnight

Lyrics by Don Hecht
Music by Alan W. Block

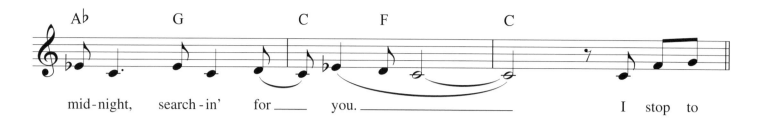

mid-night, search-in' for ____ you. _____ I stop to

Bridge

see a weep-in' wil-low ____ cry-in' on his pil-low. ____

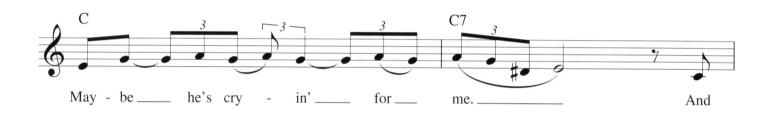

May - be ____ he's cry - in' ____ for ____ me. _____ And

as the stars turn gloom-y, ____ night winds ___ whis-per to me. I'm

To Coda ⊕

Verse

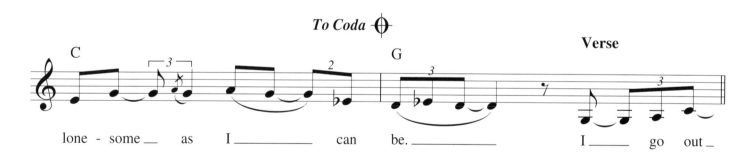

lone - some ___ as I _____ can be. _____ I ____ go out ___

____ walk-in' ____ af - ter mid-night, out ___ in the moon-light just ___

hop - in' you may be some - where out _____ walk - in' af - ter

D.S. al Coda

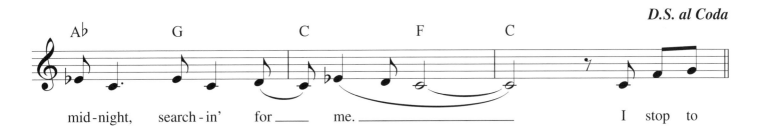

mid - night, search - in' for _____ me. _____ I stop to

Coda **Verse**

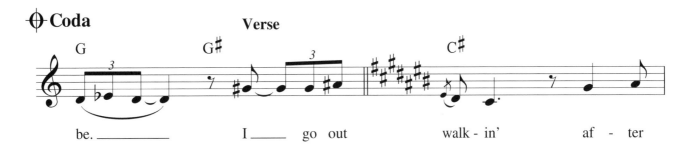

be. _____ I _____ go out walk - in' af - ter

mid - night, out _____ in the moon - light _____ just _____

hop - in' you may be some - where a - walk - in' af - ter

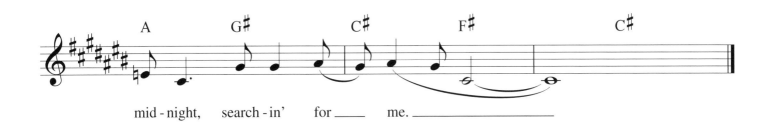

mid - night, search - in' for _____ me. _____

Pro Vocal® Series
SONGBOOK & SOUND-ALIKE CD
SING 8 CHART-TOPPING SONGS WITH A PROFESSIONAL BAND

Whether you're a karaoke singer or an auditioning professional, the Pro Vocal® series is for you! Each book contains the lyrics, melody, and chord symbols for eight hit songs. The CD contains demos for listening, and separate backing tracks so you can sing along. The CD is playable on any CD player, but it is also enhanced so PC and Mac computer users can adjust the recording to any pitch without changing the tempo! Perfect for home rehearsal, parties, auditions, corporate events, and gigs without a backup band.

ELVIS PRESLEY – VOLUME 1
Blue Suede Shoes • Can't Help Falling in Love • Don't Be Cruel (To a Heart That's True) • Good Luck Charm • I Want You, I Need You, I Love You • Love Me • (Let Me Be Your) Teddy Bear • Treat Me Nice.
00740333 ....$14.95

BROADWAY SONGS
WOMEN'S EDITION
A Change in Me (Beauty and the Beast) • I Can Hear the Bells (Hairspray) • Memory (Cats) • On My Own (Les Misérables) • Someone like You (Jekyll & Hyde) • There Are Worse Things I Could Do (Grease) • Without You (Rent).
00740247 ....$14.95

MEN'S EDITION
Alone at the Drive-In Movie (Grease) • Any Dream Will Do (Joseph and the Amazing Technicolor® Dreamcoat) • Bring Him Home (Les Misérables) • Elaborate Lives (Aida) • Seasons of Love (Rent) • They Live in You (Disney Presents The Lion King: The Broadway Musical) • This Is the Moment (Jekyll & Hyde) • Why God Why? (Miss Saigon).
00740248 ....$14.95

CHRISTMAS STANDARDS
Each song is in the style of the artist listed.

WOMEN'S EDITION
Frosty the Snow Man (Patti Page) • Let It Snow! Let It Snow! Let It Snow! (Lena Horne) • Merry Christmas, Darling (Carpenters) • My Favorite Things (Barbra Streisand) • Rockin' Around the Christmas Tree (Brenda Lee) • Rudolph the Red-Nosed Reindeer (Ella Fitzgerald) • Santa Baby (Eartha Kitt) • Santa Claus Is Comin' to Town (The Andrews Sisters).
00740299 ....$12.95

MEN'S EDITION
Blue Christmas (Elvis Presley) • The Christmas Song (Chestnuts Roasting on an Open Fire) (Nat King Cole) • The Christmas Waltz (Frank Sinatra) • Here Comes Santa Claus (Right down Santa Claus Lane) (Gene Autry) • (There's No Place Like) Home for the Holidays (Perry Como) • I'll Be Home for Christmas (Bing Crosby) • Let It Snow! Let It Snow! Let It Snow! (Vaughn Monroe) • Silver Bells (Ray Conniff).
00740298 ....$14.95

CONTEMPORARY HITS
WOMEN'S EDITION
Beautiful (Christina Aguilera) • Breathe (Faith Hill) • Complicated (Avril Lavigne) • Don't Know Why (Norah Jones) • Fallin' (Alicia Keys) • The Game of Love (Santana feat. Michelle Branch) • I Hope You Dance (Lee Ann Womack with Sons of the Desert) • My Heart Will Go On (Celine Dion).
00740246 ....$14.95

MEN'S EDITION
Drive (Incubus) • Drops of Jupiter (Tell Me) (Train) • Fly Away (Lenny Kravitz) • Hanging by a Moment (Lifehouse) • Iris (Goo Goo Dolls) • Smooth (Santana feat. Rob Thomas) • 3 AM (Matchbox 20) • Wherever You Will Go (The Calling).
00740251 ....$14.95

DISCO FEVER
WOMEN'S EDITION
Boogie Oogie Oogie (A Taste of Honey) • Funkytown (Lipps Inc.) • Hot Stuff (Donna Summer) • I Will Survive (Gloria Gaynor) • It's Raining Men (The Weather Girls) • Le Freak (Chic) • Turn the Beat Around (Vicki Sue Robinson) • We Are Family (Sister Sledge).
00740281 ....$12.95

MEN'S EDITION
Boogie Fever (The Sylvers) • Da Ya Think I'm Sexy (Rod Stewart) • Get Down Tonight (KC and the Sunshine Band) • Love Rollercoaster (Ohio Players) • Stayin' Alive (The Bee Gees) • Super Freak (Rick James) • That's the Way (I Like It) (KC and the Sunshine Band) • Y.M.C.A. (Village People).
00740282 ....$12.95

'80s GOLD
WOMEN'S EDITION
Call Me (Blondie) • Flashdance ... What a Feeling (Irene Cara) • Girls Just Want to Have Fun (Cyndi Lauper) • How Will I Know (Whitney Houston) • Material Girl (Madonna) • Mickey (Toni Basil) • Straight Up (Paula Abdul) • Walking on Sunshine (Katrina and the Waves).
00740277 ....$12.95

MEN'S EDITION
Every Breath You Take (The Police) • Heart and Soul (Huey Lewis) • Hurts So Good (John "Cougar") • It's Still Rock and Roll to Me (Billy Joel) • Jessie's Girl (Rick Springfield) • Maneater (Hall & Oates) • Summer of '69 (Bryan Adams) • You Give Love a Bad Name (Bon Jovi).
00740278 ....$12.95

JAZZ STANDARDS
Great jazz classics, each in the style of the artist listed.

WOMEN'S EDITION
Bye Bye Blackbird (Carmen McRae) • Come Rain or Come Shine (Judy Garland) • Fever (Peggy Lee) • The Girl from Ipanema (Astrud Gilberto) • Lullaby of Birdland (Ella Fitzgerald) • My Funny Valentine (Sarah Vaughan) • Stormy Weather (Keeps Rainin' All the Time) (Lena Horne) • Tenderly (Rosemary Clooney).
00740249 ....$14.95

MEN'S EDITION
Ain't Misbehavin' (Louis Armstrong) • Don't Get Around Much Anymore (Tony Bennett) • Fly Me to the Moon (In Other Words) (Frank Sinatra) • Georgia on My Mind (Ray Charles) • I've Got You Under My Skin (Mel Torme) • Misty (Johnny Mathis) • My One and Only Love (Johnny Hartman) • Route 66 (Nat King Cole).
00740250 ....$14.95

Prices, contents, & availability subject to change without notice.

R&B SUPER HITS
WOMEN'S EDITION
Baby Love (The Supremes) • Dancing in the Street (Martha & The Vandellas) • I'm So Excited (Pointer Sisters) • Lady Marmalade (Patty LaBelle) • Midnight Train to Georgia (Gladys Knight & The Pips) • Rescue Me (Fontella Bass) • Respect (Aretha Franklin) • What's Love Got to Do with It (Tina Turner).
00740279 ....$12.95

MEN'S EDITION
Brick House (Commodores) • I Can't Help Myself (Sugar Pie, Honey Bunch) (The Four Tops) • I Got You (I Feel Good) (James Brown) • In the Midnight Hour (Wilson Pickett) • Let's Get It On (Marvin Gaye) • My Girl (The Temptations) • Shining Star (Earth, Wind & Fire) • Superstition (Stevie Wonder).
00740280 ....$12.95

WEDDING GEMS
WOMEN'S EDITION
Grow Old with Me (Mary Chapin Carpenter) • How Beautiful (Twila Paris) • The Power of Love (Celine Dion) • Save the Best for Last (Vanessa Williams) • We've Only Just Begun (Carpenters) • When You Say Nothing at All (Alison Krauss & Union Station) • You Light up My Life (Debby Boone) • You Needed Me (Anne Murray).
00740309 Book/CD Pack $12.95

MEN'S EDITION
Back at One (Brian McKnight) • Butterfly Kisses (Bob Carlisle) • Here and Now (Luther Vandross) • I Will Be Here (Steven Curtis Chapman) • In My Life (The Beatles) • The Keeper of the Stars (Tracy Byrd) • Longer (Dan Fogelberg) • You Raise Me Up (Josh Groban).
00740310 Book/CD Pack $12.95

DUETS EDITION
Don't Know Much (Aaron Neville & Linda Ronstadt) • Endless Love (Diana Ross & Lionel Richie) • From This Moment On (Shania Twain & Bryan White) • I Finally Found Someone (Barbra Streisand & Bryan Adams) • I Pledge My Love (Peaches & Herb) • Nobody Loves Me like You Do (Anne Murray & Dave Loggins) • Tonight, I Celebrate My Love (Peabo Bryson & Roberta Flack) • Up Where We Belong (Joe Cocker & Jennifer Warnes).
00740311 ....$12.95

ANDREW LLOYD WEBBER
WOMEN'S EDITION
All I Ask of You • As If We Never Said Goodbye • Don't Cry for Me Argentina • I Don't Know How to Love Him • Memory • Unexpected Song • Wishing You Were Somehow Here Again • With One Look.
00740348 ....$14.95

MEN'S EDITION
All I Ask of You • Any Dream Will Do • I Only Want to Say (Gethsemane) • Love Changes Everything • Memory • The Music of the Night • No Matter What • On This Night of a Thousand Stars.
00740349 ....$14.95

THE SINGER'S MUSICAL THEATRE ANTHOLOGY

THE WORLD'S MOST TRUSTED SOURCE FOR GREAT THEATRE LITERATURE FOR SINGING ACTORS

Compiled and Edited by Richard Walters

The songs in this series are vocal essentials from classic and contemporary shows – ideal for the auditioning, practicing or performing vocalist. Each of the eighteen books contains songs chosen because of their appropriateness to that particular voice type. All selections are in their authentic form, excerpted from the original vocal scores. Each volume features notes about the shows and songs. There is no duplication between volumes.

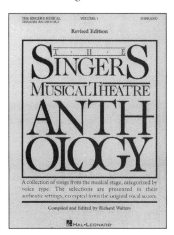   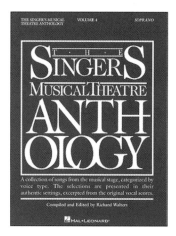

VOLUME 1

SOPRANO
(REVISED EDITION)

47 songs: Where or When • If I Loved You • Goodnight, My Someone • My Funny Valentine • Smoke Gets in Your Eyes • Barbara Song • Till There Was You • Falling in Love with Love • I Could Have Danced All Night • and many more.
00361071 Book Only $19.95
00740227 2 Accompaniment CDs...$22.95

MEZZO-SOPRANO/BELTER
(REVISED EDITION)

39 songs: Anyone Can Whistle • Broadway Baby • Doin' What Comes Naturally • Don't Cry for Me Argentina • Don't Tell Mama • How Are Things in Glocca Morra? • Losing My Mind • Send in the Clowns • and more.
00361072 Book Only $19.95
00740230 2 Accompaniment CDs...$22.95

TENOR
(REVISED EDITION)

40 songs: Being Alive • Johanna • King Herod's Song • Stranger in Paradise • On the Street Where You Live • Younger Than Springtime • Lonely House • Not While I'm Around • Wish You Were Here • and more.
00361073 Book Only $19.95
00740233 2 Accompaniment CDs...$22.95

BARITONE/BASS
(REVISED EDITION)

39 songs: Camelot • C'est Moi • September Song • The Impossible Dream • Lonely Room • Marian the Librarian • Ol' Man River • Soliloquy • Some Enchanted Evening • and more.
00361074 Book Only $19.95
00740236 2 Accompaniment CDs...$22.95

DUETS

21 songs: Too Many Mornings • We Kiss in a Shadow • People Will Say We're in Love • Bess You Is My Woman • Make Believe • more.
00361075 Book Only $17.95
00740239 2 Accompaniment CDs...$22.95

VOLUME 2

SOPRANO
(REVISED EDITION)

42 songs: And This Is My Beloved • How Could I Ever Know • If I Were a Bell • Moonfall • I'll Know • Take Me to the World • The Sound of Music • Unusual Way • Warm All Over • and more.
00747066 Book Only $19.95
00740228 2 Accompaniment CDs...$22.95

MEZZO-SOPRANO/BELTER
(REVISED EDITION)

38 songs: You're the Top • The Party's Over • Adelaide's Lament • I Dreamed a Dream • As Long as He Needs Me • On My Own • I Can Cook Too • If He Walked Into My Life • Never Never Land • Small World • Tell Me on a Sunday • and more.
00747031 Book Only $19.95
00740231 2 Accompaniment CDs...$22.95

TENOR

42 songs: Miracles of Miracles • Sit Down, You're Rockin' the Boat • Bring Him Home • Music of the Night • Close Every Door • All Good Gifts • Anthem • I Belive In You • This Is the Moment • Willkommen • Alone at the Drive-In Movie.
00747032 Book Only $19.95
00740234 2 Accompaniment CDs...$22.95

BARITONE/BASS

40 songs: This Can't Be Love • Bye, Bye Baby • The Surrey with the Fringe on Top • Empty Chairs at Empty Tables • I've Grown Accustomed to Her Face • Stars • My Defenses Are Down • and more.
00747033 Book Only $19.95
00740237 2 Accompaniment CDs...$22.95

DUETS

30 duets, including songs from *Aida, Cabaret, Chicago, Guys and Dolls, Hairspray, The Last Five Years, The Phantom of the Opera, The Producers, Show Boat, Spamalot, Wicked* and more.
00740331 Book Only $19.95
00740240 2 Accompaniment CDs...$22.95

VOLUME 3

SOPRANO

40 songs: Getting to Know You • In My Life • My Favorite Things • Once You Lose Your Heart • Someone to Watch over Me • Think of Me • Whistle Down the Wind • Wishing You Were Somehow Here Again • Wouldn't It Be Loverly • and more.
00740122 Book Only $19.95
00740229 2 Accompaniment CDs...$22.95

MEZZO SOPRANO/BELTER

41 songs: As If We Never Said Goodbye • But Not for Me • Everything's Coming up Roses • I Ain't Down Yet • Maybe This Time • My Heart Belongs to Daddy • Someone like You • Stepsisters' Lament • The Ladies Who Lunch • You Can't Get a Man with a Gun • many more.
00740123 Book Only $19.95
00740232 2 Accompaniment CDs...$22.95

TENOR

35 songs: Almost Like Being in Love • Any Dream Will Do • Corner of the Sky • Hey There • Mama Says • Mister Cellophane • One Song Glory • Steppin' Out with My Baby • Sunset Boulevard • What You'd Call a Dream • Your Eyes • and more.
00740124 Book Only $19.95
00740235 2 Accompaniment CDs...$22.95

BARITONE/BASS

42 songs: All I Care About • Gigi • I Confess • If I Can't Love Her • If I Sing • The Kid Inside • Les Poissons • Lucky to Be Me • Marry Me a Little • Paris by Night • Santa Fe • and more.
00740125 Book Only $19.95
00740238 2 Accompaniment CDs...$22.95

VOLUME 4

SOPRANO

40 songs: Bewitched • Children Will Listen • Home • I Have Dreamed • It's a Most Unusual Day • A Lovely Night • One Boy (Girl) • The Song Is You • Speak Low • We Kiss in a Shadow • Why Do I Love You? • Why Was I Born? • and more.
00000393 Book Only $19.95
00000397 2 Accompaniment CDs...$22.95

MEZZO SOPRANO/BELTER

37 songs: Anything but Lonely • Heaven Help My Heart • I Can Hear the Bells • I Don't Know How to Love Him • Just One Step • Life with Harold • The Man That Got Away • Popular • Roxie • Shadowland • There Are Worse Things I Could Do • The Wizard and I • and more.
00000394 Book Only $19.95
00000398 2 Accompaniment CDs...$22.95

TENOR

37 songs: Awaiting You • Dancing Through Life • Goodnight Saigon • If You Were Gay • Love Changes Everything • A Man Could Go Quite Mad • One Track Mind • Tschaikowsky (And Other Russians) • Who Am I? • You Walk with Me • and more.
00000395 Book Only $19.95
00000399 2 Accompaniment CDs...$22.95

BARITONE/BASS

40 songs: Along Came Bialy • Edelweiss • Get Me to the Church on Time • I'm Not Wearing Underwear Today • A Lot of Livin' to Do • Put on a Happy Face • Wonderful • Ya Got Trouble • and more.
00000396 Book Only $19.95
00000401 2 Accompaniment CDs...$22.95

Prices, contents, and availability are subject to change without notice.

Please visit **www.halleonard.com** for complete contents listings.

FOR MORE INFORMATION, SEE YOUR LOCAL MUSIC DEALER, OR WRITE TO:

HAL•LEONARD® CORPORATION

7777 W. BLUEMOUND RD. P.O. BOX 13819 MILWAUKEE, WI 53213

0107